This journal belongs to

· ·

Squat

Jumping rope

Plank

Jump

Sprint

Goals to reach

....

....

....

....

....

....

....

....

....

....

....

Stretching

Week from..... to.....		Mon	Tues	Wed	Thur	Fri	Sat	Sun
Squat	Mass							
	Series							
	Repetitions							
	Total volume							
Jumping rope	Duration							
Electro Stimulation	Buttock Muscle							
	Quadriceps							
	Calves							
Plank	Repetitions							
	Duration							
8 jumps, sprint 30 m, recover 15″	Repetitions							
10 jumps, maintain 10″	Repetitions							

Week from..... to.....		Mon	Tues	Wed	Thur	Fri	Sat	Sun
Squat hop	*Series*							
Step	*Series*							
	Repetitions							
Thrust up	*Series*							
	Repetitions							
Backrest without chair and multibond	*Repetitions*							
Bouncing strides	*Simple Series*							
	Hands on head Series							
	Series with charge							
Stretching	*Buttock*							
	Quadriceps							
	Calves							

Week from..... to.....		Mon	Tues	Wed	Thur	Fri	Sat	Sun
Squat	Mass							
	Series							
	Repetitions							
	Total volume							
Jumping rope	Duration							
Electro Stimulation	Buttock Muscle							
	Quadriceps							
	Calves							
Plank	Repetitions							
	Duration							
8 jumps, sprint 30 m, recover 15''	Repetitions							
10 jumps, maintain 10''	Repetitions							

Week from..... to.....		Mon	Tues	Wed	Thur	Fri	Sat	Sun
Squat hop	Series							
Step	Series							
	Repetitions							
Thrust up	Series							
	Repetitions							
Backrest without chair and multibond	Repetitions							
Bouncing strides	Simple Series							
	Hands on head Series							
	Series with charge							
Stretching	Buttock							
	Quadriceps							
	Calves							

Week from..... to.....		Mon	Tues	Wed	Thur	Fri	Sat	Sun
Squat	Mass							
	Series							
	Repetitions							
	Total volume							
Jumping rope	Duration							
Electro Stimulation	Buttock Muscle							
	Quadriceps							
	Calves							
Plank	Repetitions							
	Duration							
8 jumps, sprint 30 m, recover 15"	Repetitions							
10 jumps, maintain 10"	Repetitions							

Week from..... to.....		Mon	Tues	Wed	Thur	Fri	Sat	Sun
Squat hop	*Series*							
Step	*Series*							
	Repetitions							
Thrust up	*Series*							
	Repetitions							
Backrest without chair and multibond	*Repetitions*							
Bouncing strides	*Simple Series*							
	Hands on head Series							
	Series with charge							
Stretching	*Buttock*							
	Quadriceps							
	Calves							

Week from..... to.....		Mon	Tues	Wed	Thur	Fri	Sat	Sun
Squat	Mass							
	Series							
	Repetitions							
	Total volume							
Jumping rope	Duration							
Electro Stimulation	Buttock Muscle							
	Quadriceps							
	Calves							
Plank	Repetitions							
	Duration							
8 jumps, sprint 30 m, recover 15''	Repetitions							
10 jumps, maintain 10''	Repetitions							

Week from..... to.....		Mon	Tues	Wed	Thur	Fri	Sat	Sun
Squat hop	Series							
Step	Series							
	Repetitions							
Thrust up	Series							
	Repetitions							
Backrest without chair and multibond	Repetitions							
Bouncing strides	Simple Series							
	Hands on head Series							
	Series with charge							
Stretching	Buttock							
	Quadriceps							
	Calves							

Week from..... to.....		Mon	Tues	Wed	Thur	Fri	Sat	Sun
Squat	Mass							
	Series							
	Repetitions							
	Total volume							
Jumping rope	Duration							
Electro Stimulation	Buttock Muscle							
	Quadriceps							
	Calves							
Plank	Repetitions							
	Duration							
8 jumps, sprint 30 m, recover 15''	Repetitions							
10 jumps, maintain 10''	Repetitions							

Week from..... to.....		Mon	Tues	Wed	Thur	Fri	Sat	Sun
Squat hop	Series							
Step	Series							
	Repetitions							
Thrust up	Series							
	Repetitions							
Backrest without chair and multibond	Repetitions							
Bouncing strides	Simple Series							
	Hands on head Series							
	Series with charge							
Stretching	Buttock							
	Quadriceps							
	Calves							

Week from..... to.....		Mon	Tues	Wed	Thur	Fri	Sat	Sun
	Mass							
	Series							
Squat	Repetitions							
	Total volume							
Jumping rope	Duration							
	Buttock Muscle							
Electro Stimulation	Quadriceps							
	Calves							
	Repetitions							
Plank	Duration							
8 jumps, sprint 30 m, recover 15"	Repetitions							
10 jumps, maintain 10"	Repetitions							

Week from..... to.....		Mon	Tues	Wed	Thur	Fri	Sat	Sun
Squat hop	*Series*							
Step	*Series*							
	Repetitions							
Thrust up	*Series*							
	Repetitions							
Backrest without chair and multibond	*Repetitions*							
Bouncing strides	*Simple Series*							
	Hands on head Series							
	Series with charge							
Stretching	*Buttock*							
	Quadriceps							
	Calves							

Week from..... to.....		Mon	Tues	Wed	Thur	Fri	Sat	Sun
Squat	Mass							
	Series							
	Repetitions							
	Total volume							
Jumping rope	Duration							
Electro Stimulation	Buttock Muscle							
	Quadriceps							
	Calves							
Plank	Repetitions							
	Duration							
8 jumps, sprint 30 m, recover 15''	Repetitions							
10 jumps, maintain 10''	Repetitions							

Week from..... to.....		Mon	Tues	Wed	Thur	Fri	Sat	Sun
Squat hop	*Series*							
Step	*Series*							
	Repetitions							
Thrust up	*Series*							
	Repetitions							
Backrest without chair and multibond	*Repetitions*							
Bouncing strides	*Simple Series*							
	Hands on head Series							
	Series with charge							
Stretching	*Buttock*							
	Quadriceps							
	Calves							

Week from..... to.....		Mon	Tues	Wed	Thur	Fri	Sat	Sun
Squat	Mass							
	Series							
	Repetitions							
	Total volume							
Jumping rope	Duration							
Electro Stimulation	Buttock Muscle							
	Quadriceps							
	Calves							
Plank	Repetitions							
	Duration							
8 jumps, sprint 30 m, recover 15″	Repetitions							
10 jumps, maintain 10″	Repetitions							

Week from..... to.....		Mon	Tues	Wed	Thur	Fri	Sat	Sun
Squat hop	*Series*							
Step	*Series*							
	Repetitions							
Thrust up	*Series*							
	Repetitions							
Backrest without chair and multibond	*Repetitions*							
Bouncing strides	*Simple Series*							
	Hands on head Series							
	Series with charge							
Stretching	*Buttock*							
	Quadriceps							
	Calves							

Week from..... to.....		Mon	Tues	Wed	Thur	Fri	Sat	Sun
Squat	Mass							
	Series							
	Repetitions							
	Total volume							
Jumping rope	Duration							
Electro Stimulation	Buttock Muscle							
	Quadriceps							
	Calves							
Plank	Repetitions							
	Duration							
8 jumps, sprint 30 m, recover 15"	Repetitions							
10 jumps, maintain 10"	Repetitions							

Week from..... to.....		Mon	Tues	Wed	Thur	Fri	Sat	Sun
Squat hop	*Series*							
Step	*Series*							
	Repetitions							
Thrust up	*Series*							
	Repetitions							
Backrest without chair and multibond	*Repetitions*							
Bouncing strides	*Simple Series*							
	Hands on head Series							
	Series with charge							
Stretching	*Buttock*							
	Quadriceps							
	Calves							

Week from..... to.....		Mon	Tues	Wed	Thur	Fri	Sat	Sun
Squat	Mass							
	Series							
	Repetitions							
	Total volume							
Jumping rope	Duration							
Electro Stimulation	Buttock Muscle							
	Quadriceps							
	Calves							
Plank	Repetitions							
	Duration							
8 jumps, sprint 30 m, recover 15"	Repetitions							
10 jumps, maintain 10"	Repetitions							

Week from..... to.....		Mon	Tues	Wed	Thur	Fri	Sat	Sun
Squat hop	Series							
Step	Series							
	Repetitions							
Thrust up	Series							
	Repetitions							
Backrest without chair and multibond	Repetitions							
Bouncing strides	Simple Series							
	Hands on head Series							
	Series with charge							
Stretching	Buttock							
	Quadriceps							
	Calves							

Week from..... to.....		Mon	Tues	Wed	Thur	Fri	Sat	Sun
Squat	Mass							
	Series							
	Repetitions							
	Total volume							
Jumping rope	Duration							
Electro Stimulation	Buttock Muscle							
	Quadriceps							
	Calves							
Plank	Repetitions							
	Duration							
8 jumps, sprint 30 m, recover 15''	Repetitions							
10 jumps, maintain 10''	Repetitions							

Week from..... to.....		Mon	Tues	Wed	Thur	Fri	Sat	Sun
Squat hop	*Series*							
Step	*Series*							
	Repetitions							
Thrust up	*Series*							
	Repetitions							
Backrest without chair and multibond	*Repetitions*							
Bouncing strides	*Simple Series*							
	Hands on head Series							
	Series with charge							
Stretching	*Buttock*							
	Quadriceps							
	Calves							

Week from..... to.....		Mon	Tues	Wed	Thur	Fri	Sat	Sun
Squat	Mass							
	Series							
	Repetitions							
	Total volume							
Jumping rope	Duration							
Electro Stimulation	Buttock Muscle							
	Quadriceps							
	Calves							
Plank	Repetitions							
	Duration							
8 jumps, sprint 30 m, recover 15"	Repetitions							
10 jumps, maintain 10"	Repetitions							

Week from..... to.....		Mon	Tues	Wed	Thur	Fri	Sat	Sun
Squat hop	Series							
Step	Series							
	Repetitions							
Thrust up	Series							
	Repetitions							
Backrest without chair and multibond	Repetitions							
Bouncing strides	Simple Series							
	Hands on head Series							
	Series with charge							
Stretching	Buttock							
	Quadriceps							
	Calves							

Week from..... to.....		Mon	Tues	Wed	Thur	Fri	Sat	Sun
Squat	Mass							
	Series							
	Repetitions							
	Total volume							
Jumping rope	Duration							
Electro Stimulation	Buttock Muscle							
	Quadriceps							
	Calves							
Plank	Repetitions							
	Duration							
8 jumps, sprint 30 m, recover 15"	Repetitions							
10 jumps, maintain 10"	Repetitions							

Week from..... to.....		Mon	Tues	Wed	Thur	Fri	Sat	Sun
Squat hop	*Series*							
Step	*Series*							
	Repetitions							
Thrust up	*Series*							
	Repetitions							
Backrest without chair and multibond	*Repetitions*							
Bouncing strides	*Simple Series*							
	Hands on head Series							
	Series with charge							
Stretching	*Buttock*							
	Quadriceps							
	Calves							

Week from..... to.....		Mon	Tues	Wed	Thur	Fri	Sat	Sun
Squat	Mass							
	Series							
	Repetitions							
	Total volume							
Jumping rope	Duration							
Electro Stimulation	Buttock Muscle							
	Quadriceps							
	Calves							
Plank	Repetitions							
	Duration							
8 jumps, sprint 30 m, recover 15"	Repetitions							
10 jumps, maintain 10"	Repetitions							

Week from..... to.....		Mon	Tues	Wed	Thur	Fri	Sat	Sun
Squat hop	*Series*							
Step	*Series*							
	Repetitions							
Thrust up	*Series*							
	Repetitions							
Backrest without chair and multibond	*Repetitions*							
Bouncing strides	*Simple Series*							
	Hands on head Series							
	Series with charge							
Stretching	*Buttock*							
	Quadriceps							
	Calves							

Week from..... to.....		Mon	Tues	Wed	Thur	Fri	Sat	Sun
Squat	Mass							
	Series							
	Repetitions							
	Total volume							
Jumping rope	Duration							
Electro Stimulation	Buttock Muscle							
	Quadriceps							
	Calves							
Plank	Repetitions							
	Duration							
8 jumps, sprint 30 m, recover 15"	Repetitions							
10 jumps, maintain 10"	Repetitions							

Week from..... to.....		Mon	Tues	Wed	Thur	Fri	Sat	Sun
Squat hop	*Series*							
Step	*Series*							
	Repetitions							
Thrust up	*Series*							
	Repetitions							
Backrest without chair and multibond	*Repetitions*							
Bouncing strides	*Simple Series*							
	Hands on head Series							
	Series with charge							
Stretching	*Buttock*							
	Quadriceps							
	Calves							

Week from..... to.....		Mon	Tues	Wed	Thur	Fri	Sat	Sun
Squat	Mass							
	Series							
	Repetitions							
	Total volume							
Jumping rope	Duration							
Electro Stimulation	Buttock Muscle							
	Quadriceps							
	Calves							
Plank	Repetitions							
	Duration							
8 jumps, sprint 30 m, recover 15"	Repetitions							
10 jumps, maintain 10"	Repetitions							

Week from..... to.....		Mon	Tues	Wed	Thur	Fri	Sat	Sun
Squat hop	*Series*							
Step	*Series*							
	Repetitions							
Thrust up	*Series*							
	Repetitions							
Backrest without chair and multibond	*Repetitions*							
Bouncing strides	*Simple Series*							
	Hands on head Series							
	Series with charge							
Stretching	*Buttock*							
	Quadriceps							
	Calves							

Week from..... to.....		Mon	Tues	Wed	Thur	Fri	Sat	Sun
Squat	Mass							
	Series							
	Repetitions							
	Total volume							
Jumping rope	Duration							
Electro Stimulation	Buttock Muscle							
	Quadriceps							
	Calves							
Plank	Repetitions							
	Duration							
8 jumps, sprint 30 m, recover 15″	Repetitions							
10 jumps, maintain 10″	Repetitions							

Week from..... to.....		Mon	Tues	Wed	Thur	Fri	Sat	Sun
Squat hop	Series							
Step	Series							
	Repetitions							
Thrust up	Series							
	Repetitions							
Backrest without chair and multibond	Repetitions							
Bouncing strides	Simple Series							
	Hands on head Series							
	Series with charge							
Stretching	Buttock							
	Quadriceps							
	Calves							

Week from..... to.....		Mon	Tues	Wed	Thur	Fri	Sat	Sun
Squat	Mass							
	Series							
	Repetitions							
	Total volume							
Jumping rope	Duration							
Electro Stimulation	Buttock Muscle							
	Quadriceps							
	Calves							
Plank	Repetitions							
	Duration							
8 jumps, sprint 30 m, recover 15"	Repetitions							
10 jumps, maintain 10"	Repetitions							

Week from..... to.....		Mon	Tues	Wed	Thur	Fri	Sat	Sun
Squat hop	*Series*							
Step	*Series*							
	Repetitions							
Thrust up	*Series*							
	Repetitions							
Backrest without chair and multibond	*Repetitions*							
Bouncing strides	*Simple Series*							
	Hands on head Series							
	Series with charge							
Stretching	*Buttock*							
	Quadriceps							
	Calves							

Week from..... to.....		Mon	Tues	Wed	Thur	Fri	Sat	Sun
Squat	Mass							
	Series							
	Repetitions							
	Total volume							
Jumping rope	Duration							
Electro Stimulation	Buttock Muscle							
	Quadriceps							
	Calves							
Plank	Repetitions							
	Duration							
8 jumps, sprint 30 m, recover 15"	Repetitions							
10 jumps, maintain 10"	Repetitions							

Week from..... to.....		Mon	Tues	Wed	Thur	Fri	Sat	Sun
Squat hop	*Series*							
Step	*Series*							
	Repetitions							
Thrust up	*Series*							
	Repetitions							
Backrest without chair and multibond	*Repetitions*							
Bouncing strides	*Simple Series*							
	Hands on head Series							
	Series with charge							
Stretching	*Buttock*							
	Quadriceps							
	Calves							

Week from..... to.....		Mon	Tues	Wed	Thur	Fri	Sat	Sun
Squat	Mass							
	Series							
	Repetitions							
	Total volume							
Jumping rope	Duration							
Electro Stimulation	Buttock Muscle							
	Quadriceps							
	Calves							
Plank	Repetitions							
	Duration							
8 jumps, sprint 30 m, recover 15"	Repetitions							
10 jumps, maintain 10"	Repetitions							

Week from..... to.....		Mon	Tues	Wed	Thur	Fri	Sat	Sun
Squat hop	Series							
Step	Series							
	Repetitions							
Thrust up	Series							
	Repetitions							
Backrest without chair and multibond	Repetitions							
Bouncing strides	Simple Series							
	Hands on head Series							
	Series with charge							
Stretching	Buttock							
	Quadriceps							
	Calves							

Week from..... to.....		Mon	Tues	Wed	Thur	Fri	Sat	Sun
Squat	Mass							
	Series							
	Repetitions							
	Total volume							
Jumping rope	Duration							
Electro Stimulation	Buttock Muscle							
	Quadriceps							
	Calves							
Plank	Repetitions							
	Duration							
8 jumps, sprint 30 m, recover 15″	Repetitions							
10 jumps, maintain 10″	Repetitions							

Week from..... to.....		Mon	Tues	Wed	Thur	Fri	Sat	Sun
Squat hop	Series							
Step	Series							
	Repetitions							
Thrust up	Series							
	Repetitions							
Backrest without chair and multibond	Repetitions							
Bouncing strides	Simple Series							
	Hands on head Series							
	Series with charge							
Stretching	Buttock							
	Quadriceps							
	Calves							

Week from..... to.....		Mon	Tues	Wed	Thur	Fri	Sat	Sun
Squat	Mass							
	Series							
	Repetitions							
	Total volume							
Jumping rope	Duration							
Electro Stimulation	Buttock Muscle							
	Quadriceps							
	Calves							
Plank	Repetitions							
	Duration							
8 jumps, sprint 30 m, recover 15''	Repetitions							
10 jumps, maintain 10''	Repetitions							

Week from..... to.....		Mon	Tues	Wed	Thur	Fri	Sat	Sun
Squat hop	*Series*							
Step	*Series*							
	Repetitions							
Thrust up	*Series*							
	Repetitions							
Backrest without chair and multibond	*Repetitions*							
Bouncing strides	*Simple Series*							
	Hands on head Series							
	Series with charge							
Stretching	*Buttock*							
	Quadriceps							
	Calves							

Week from..... to.....		Mon	Tues	Wed	Thur	Fri	Sat	Sun
Squat	Mass							
	Series							
	Repetitions							
	Total volume							
Jumping rope	Duration							
Electro Stimulation	Buttock Muscle							
	Quadriceps							
	Calves							
Plank	Repetitions							
	Duration							
8 jumps, sprint 30 m, recover 15"	Repetitions							
10 jumps, maintain 10"	Repetitions							

Week from..... to.....		Mon	Tues	Wed	Thur	Fri	Sat	Sun
Squat hop	*Series*							
Step	*Series*							
	Repetitions							
Thrust up	*Series*							
	Repetitions							
Backrest without chair and multibond	*Repetitions*							
Bouncing strides	*Simple Series*							
	Hands on head Series							
	Series with charge							
Stretching	*Buttock*							
	Quadriceps							
	Calves							

Week from..... to.....		Mon	Tues	Wed	Thur	Fri	Sat	Sun
Squat	Mass							
	Series							
	Repetitions							
	Total volume							
Jumping rope	Duration							
Electro Stimulation	Buttock Muscle							
	Quadriceps							
	Calves							
Plank	Repetitions							
	Duration							
8 jumps, sprint 30 m, recover 15''	Repetitions							
10 jumps, maintain 10''	Repetitions							

Week from..... to.....		Mon	Tues	Wed	Thur	Fri	Sat	Sun
Squat hop	Series							
Step	Series							
	Repetitions							
Thrust up	Series							
	Repetitions							
Backrest without chair and multibond	Repetitions							
Bouncing strides	Simple Series							
	Hands on head Series							
	Series with charge							
Stretching	Buttock							
	Quadriceps							
	Calves							

Week from..... to.....		Mon	Tues	Wed	Thur	Fri	Sat	Sun
Squat	Mass							
	Series							
	Repetitions							
	Total volume							
Jumping rope	Duration							
Electro Stimulation	Buttock Muscle							
	Quadriceps							
	Calves							
Plank	Repetitions							
	Duration							
8 jumps, sprint 30 m, recover 15"	Repetitions							
10 jumps, maintain 10"	Repetitions							

Week from..... to.....		Mon	Tues	Wed	Thur	Fri	Sat	Sun
Squat hop	*Series*							
Step	*Series*							
	Repetitions							
Thrust up	*Series*							
	Repetitions							
Backrest without chair and multibond	*Repetitions*							
Bouncing strides	*Simple Series*							
	Hands on head Series							
	Series with charge							
Stretching	*Buttock*							
	Quadriceps							
	Calves							

Week from..... to.....		Mon	Tues	Wed	Thur	Fri	Sat	Sun
Squat	Mass							
	Series							
	Repetitions							
	Total volume							
Jumping rope	Duration							
Electro Stimulation	Buttock Muscle							
	Quadriceps							
	Calves							
Plank	Repetitions							
	Duration							
8 jumps, sprint 30 m, recover 15"	Repetitions							
10 jumps, maintain 10"	Repetitions							

Week from..... to.....		Mon	Tues	Wed	Thur	Fri	Sat	Sun
Squat hop	Series							
Step	Series							
	Repetitions							
Thrust up	Series							
	Repetitions							
Backrest without chair and multibond	Repetitions							
Bouncing strides	Simple Series							
	Hands on head Series							
	Series with charge							
Stretching	Buttock							
	Quadriceps							
	Calves							

Week from..... to.....		Mon	Tues	Wed	Thur	Fri	Sat	Sun
Squat	Mass							
	Series							
	Repetitions							
	Total volume							
Jumping rope	Duration							
Electro Stimulation	Buttock Muscle							
	Quadriceps							
	Calves							
Plank	Repetitions							
	Duration							
8 jumps, sprint 30 m, recover 15"	Repetitions							
10 jumps, maintain 10"	Repetitions							

Week from..... to.....		Mon	Tues	Wed	Thur	Fri	Sat	Sun
Squat hop	Series							
Step	Series							
	Repetitions							
Thrust up	Series							
	Repetitions							
Backrest without chair and multibond	Repetitions							
Bouncing strides	Simple Series							
	Hands on head Series							
	Series with charge							
Stretching	Buttock							
	Quadriceps							
	Calves							

Week from..... to.....		Mon	Tues	Wed	Thur	Fri	Sat	Sun
Squat	Mass							
	Series							
	Repetitions							
	Total volume							
Jumping rope	Duration							
Electro Stimulation	Buttock Muscle							
	Quadriceps							
	Calves							
Plank	Repetitions							
	Duration							
8 jumps, sprint 30 m, recover 15"	Repetitions							
10 jumps, maintain 10"	Repetitions							

Week from..... to.....		Mon	Tues	Wed	Thur	Fri	Sat	Sun
Squat hop	*Series*							
Step	*Series*							
	Repetitions							
Thrust up	*Series*							
	Repetitions							
Backrest without chair and multibond	*Repetitions*							
Bouncing strides	*Simple Series*							
	Hands on head Series							
	Series with charge							
Stretching	*Buttock*							
	Quadriceps							
	Calves							

Week from..... to.....		Mon	Tues	Wed	Thur	Fri	Sat	Sun
Squat	Mass							
	Series							
	Repetitions							
	Total volume							
Jumping rope	Duration							
Electro Stimulation	Buttock Muscle							
	Quadriceps							
	Calves							
Plank	Repetitions							
	Duration							
8 jumps, sprint 30 m, recover 15"	Repetitions							
10 jumps, maintain 10"	Repetitions							

Week from..... to.....		Mon	Tues	Wed	Thur	Fri	Sat	Sun
Squat hop	*Series*							
Step	*Series*							
	Repetitions							
Thrust up	*Series*							
	Repetitions							
Backrest without chair and multibond	*Repetitions*							
Bouncing strides	*Simple Series*							
	Hands on head Series							
	Series with charge							
Stretching	*Buttock*							
	Quadriceps							
	Calves							

Week from..... to.....		Mon	Tues	Wed	Thur	Fri	Sat	Sun
Squat	Mass							
	Series							
	Repetitions							
	Total volume							
Jumping rope	Duration							
Electro Stimulation	Buttock Muscle							
	Quadriceps							
	Calves							
Plank	Repetitions							
	Duration							
8 jumps, sprint 30 m, recover 15''	Repetitions							
10 jumps, maintain 10''	Repetitions							

Week from..... to.....		Mon	Tues	Wed	Thur	Fri	Sat	Sun
Squat hop	*Series*							
Step	*Series*							
	Repetitions							
Thrust up	*Series*							
	Repetitions							
Backrest without chair and multibond	*Repetitions*							
Bouncing strides	*Simple Series*							
	Hands on head Series							
	Series with charge							
Stretching	*Buttock*							
	Quadriceps							
	Calves							

Week from..... to.....		Mon	Tues	Wed	Thur	Fri	Sat	Sun
Squat	Mass							
	Series							
	Repetitions							
	Total volume							
Jumping rope	Duration							
Electro Stimulation	Buttock Muscle							
	Quadriceps							
	Calves							
Plank	Repetitions							
	Duration							
8 jumps, sprint 30 m, recover 15"	Repetitions							
10 jumps, maintain 10"	Repetitions							

Week from..... to.....		Mon	Tues	Wed	Thur	Fri	Sat	Sun
Squat hop	*Series*							
Step	*Series*							
	Repetitions							
Thrust up	*Series*							
	Repetitions							
Backrest without chair and multibond	*Repetitions*							
Bouncing strides	*Simple Series*							
	Hands on head Series							
	Series with charge							
Stretching	*Buttock*							
	Quadriceps							
	Calves							

Week from..... to.....		Mon	Tues	Wed	Thur	Fri	Sat	Sun
Squat	Mass							
	Series							
	Repetitions							
	Total volume							
Jumping rope	Duration							
Electro Stimulation	Buttock Muscle							
	Quadriceps							
	Calves							
Plank	Repetitions							
	Duration							
8 jumps, sprint 30 m, recover 15″	Repetitions							
10 jumps, maintain 10″	Repetitions							

Week from..... to.....		Mon	Tues	Wed	Thur	Fri	Sat	Sun
Squat hop	Series							
Step	Series							
	Repetitions							
Thrust up	Series							
	Repetitions							
Backrest without chair and multibond	Repetitions							
Bouncing strides	Simple Series							
	Hands on head Series							
	Series with charge							
Stretching	Buttock							
	Quadriceps							
	Calves							

Week from..... to.....		Mon	Tues	Wed	Thur	Fri	Sat	Sun
Squat	Mass							
	Series							
	Repetitions							
	Total volume							
Jumping rope	Duration							
Electro Stimulation	Buttock Muscle							
	Quadriceps							
	Calves							
Plank	Repetitions							
	Duration							
8 jumps, sprint 30 m, recover 15"	Repetitions							
10 jumps, maintain 10"	Repetitions							

Week from..... to.....		Mon	Tues	Wed	Thur	Fri	Sat	Sun
Squat hop	Series							
Step	Series							
	Repetitions							
Thrust up	Series							
	Repetitions							
Backrest without chair and multibond	Repetitions							
Bouncing strides	Simple Series							
	Hands on head Series							
	Series with charge							
Stretching	Buttock							
	Quadriceps							
	Calves							

Week from..... to.....		Mon	Tues	Wed	Thur	Fri	Sat	Sun
Squat	Mass							
	Series							
	Repetitions							
	Total volume							
Jumping rope	Duration							
Electro Stimulation	Buttock Muscle							
	Quadriceps							
	Calves							
Plank	Repetitions							
	Duration							
8 jumps, sprint 30 m, recover 15″	Repetitions							
10 jumps, maintain 10″	Repetitions							

Week from..... to.....		Mon	Tues	Wed	Thur	Fri	Sat	Sun
Squat hop	Series							
Step	Series							
	Repetitions							
Thrust up	Series							
	Repetitions							
Backrest without chair and multibond	Repetitions							
Bouncing strides	Simple Series							
	Hands on head Series							
	Series with charge							
Stretching	Buttock							
	Quadriceps							
	Calves							

Week from..... to.....		Mon	Tues	Wed	Thur	Fri	Sat	Sun
Squat	Mass							
	Series							
	Repetitions							
	Total volume							
Jumping rope	Duration							
Electro Stimulation	Buttock Muscle							
	Quadriceps							
	Calves							
Plank	Repetitions							
	Duration							
8 jumps, sprint 30 m, recover 15''	Repetitions							
10 jumps, maintain 10''	Repetitions							

Week from..... to.....		Mon	Tues	Wed	Thur	Fri	Sat	Sun
Squat hop	Series							
Step	Series							
	Repetitions							
Thrust up	Series							
	Repetitions							
Backrest without chair and multibond	Repetitions							
Bouncing strides	Simple Series							
	Hands on head Series							
	Series with charge							
Stretching	Buttock							
	Quadriceps							
	Calves							

Week from..... to.....		Mon	Tues	Wed	Thur	Fri	Sat	Sun
Squat	Mass							
	Series							
	Repetitions							
	Total volume							
Jumping rope	Duration							
Electro Stimulation	Buttock Muscle							
	Quadriceps							
	Calves							
Plank	Repetitions							
	Duration							
8 jumps, sprint 30 m, recover 15"	Repetitions							
10 jumps, maintain 10"	Repetitions							

Week from..... to.....		Mon	Tues	Wed	Thur	Fri	Sat	Sun
Squat hop	*Series*							
Step	*Series*							
	Repetitions							
Thrust up	*Series*							
	Repetitions							
Backrest without chair and multibond	*Repetitions*							
Bouncing strides	*Simple Series*							
	Hands on head Series							
	Series with charge							
Stretching	*Buttock*							
	Quadriceps							
	Calves							

Week from..... to.....		Mon	Tues	Wed	Thur	Fri	Sat	Sun
Squat	Mass							
	Series							
	Repetitions							
	Total volume							
Jumping rope	Duration							
Electro Stimulation	Buttock Muscle							
	Quadriceps							
	Calves							
Plank	Repetitions							
	Duration							
8 jumps, sprint 30 m, recover 15''	Repetitions							
10 jumps, maintain 10''	Repetitions							

Week from..... to.....		Mon	Tues	Wed	Thur	Fri	Sat	Sun
Squat hop	*Series*							
Step	*Series*							
	Repetitions							
Thrust up	*Series*							
	Repetitions							
Backrest without chair and multibond	*Repetitions*							
Bouncing strides	*Simple Series*							
	Hands on head Series							
	Series with charge							
Stretching	*Buttock*							
	Quadriceps							
	Calves							

Week from..... to.....		Mon	Tues	Wed	Thur	Fri	Sat	Sun
Squat	Mass							
	Series							
	Repetitions							
	Total volume							
Jumping rope	Duration							
Electro Stimulation	Buttock Muscle							
	Quadriceps							
	Calves							
Plank	Repetitions							
	Duration							
8 jumps, sprint 30 m, recover 15''	Repetitions							
10 jumps, maintain 10''	Repetitions							

Week from..... to.....		Mon	Tues	Wed	Thur	Fri	Sat	Sun
Squat hop	Series							
Step	Series							
	Repetitions							
Thrust up	Series							
	Repetitions							
Backrest without chair and multibond	Repetitions							
Bouncing strides	Simple Series							
	Hands on head Series							
	Series with charge							
Stretching	Buttock							
	Quadriceps							
	Calves							

Week from..... to.....		Mon	Tues	Wed	Thur	Fri	Sat	Sun
Squat	Mass							
	Series							
	Repetitions							
	Total volume							
Jumping rope	Duration							
Electro Stimulation	Buttock Muscle							
	Quadriceps							
	Calves							
Plank	Repetitions							
	Duration							
8 jumps, sprint 30 m, recover 15″	Repetitions							
10 jumps, maintain 10″	Repetitions							

Week from..... to.....		Mon	Tues	Wed	Thur	Fri	Sat	Sun
Squat hop	Series							
Step	Series							
	Repetitions							
Thrust up	Series							
	Repetitions							
Backrest without chair and multibond	Repetitions							
Bouncing strides	Simple Series							
	Hands on head Series							
	Series with charge							
Stretching	Buttock							
	Quadriceps							
	Calves							

Week from..... to.....		Mon	Tues	Wed	Thur	Fri	Sat	Sun
Squat	Mass							
	Series							
	Repetitions							
	Total volume							
Jumping rope	Duration							
Electro Stimulation	Buttock Muscle							
	Quadriceps							
	Calves							
Plank	Repetitions							
	Duration							
8 jumps, sprint 30 m, recover 15''	Repetitions							
10 jumps, maintain 10''	Repetitions							

Week from..... to.....		Mon	Tues	Wed	Thur	Fri	Sat	Sun
Squat hop	*Series*							
Step	*Series*							
	Repetitions							
Thrust up	*Series*							
	Repetitions							
Backrest without chair and multibond	*Repetitions*							
Bouncing strides	*Simple Series*							
	Hands on head Series							
	Series with charge							
Stretching	*Buttock*							
	Quadriceps							
	Calves							

Week from..... to.....		Mon	Tues	Wed	Thur	Fri	Sat	Sun
Squat	Mass							
	Series							
	Repetitions							
	Total volume							
Jumping rope	Duration							
Electro Stimulation	Buttock Muscle							
	Quadriceps							
	Calves							
Plank	Repetitions							
	Duration							
8 jumps, sprint 30 m, recover 15''	Repetitions							
10 jumps, maintain 10''	Repetitions							

Week from..... to.....		Mon	Tues	Wed	Thur	Fri	Sat	Sun
Squat hop	Series							
Step	Series							
	Repetitions							
Thrust up	Series							
	Repetitions							
Backrest without chair and multibond	Repetitions							
Bouncing strides	Simple Series							
	Hands on head Series							
	Series with charge							
Stretching	Buttock							
	Quadriceps							
	Calves							

Week from..... to.....		Mon	Tues	Wed	Thur	Fri	Sat	Sun
Squat	Mass							
	Series							
	Repetitions							
	Total volume							
Jumping rope	Duration							
Electro Stimulation	Buttock Muscle							
	Quadriceps							
	Calves							
Plank	Repetitions							
	Duration							
8 jumps, sprint 30 m, recover 15"	Repetitions							
10 jumps, maintain 10"	Repetitions							

Week from..... to.....		Mon	Tues	Wed	Thur	Fri	Sat	Sun
Squat hop	*Series*							
Step	*Series*							
	Repetitions							
Thrust up	*Series*							
	Repetitions							
Backrest without chair and multibond	*Repetitions*							
Bouncing strides	*Simple Series*							
	Hands on head Series							
	Series with charge							
Stretching	*Buttock*							
	Quadriceps							
	Calves							

Week from..... to.....		Mon	Tues	Wed	Thur	Fri	Sat	Sun
Squat	Mass							
	Series							
	Repetitions							
	Total volume							
Jumping rope	Duration							
Electro Stimulation	Buttock Muscle							
	Quadriceps							
	Calves							
Plank	Repetitions							
	Duration							
8 jumps, sprint 30 m, recover 15"	Repetitions							
10 jumps, maintain 10"	Repetitions							

Week from..... to.....		Mon	Tues	Wed	Thur	Fri	Sat	Sun
Squat hop	Series							
Step	Series							
	Repetitions							
Thrust up	Series							
	Repetitions							
Backrest without chair and multibond	Repetitions							
Bouncing strides	Simple Series							
	Hands on head Series							
	Series with charge							
Stretching	Buttock							
	Quadriceps							
	Calves							

Week from..... to.....		Mon	Tues	Wed	Thur	Fri	Sat	Sun
Squat	Mass							
	Series							
	Repetitions							
	Total volume							
Jumping rope	Duration							
Electro Stimulation	Buttock Muscle							
	Quadriceps							
	Calves							
Plank	Repetitions							
	Duration							
8 jumps, sprint 30 m, recover 15''	Repetitions							
10 jumps, maintain 10''	Repetitions							

Week from..... to.....		Mon	Tues	Wed	Thur	Fri	Sat	Sun
Squat hop	Series							
Step	Series							
	Repetitions							
Thrust up	Series							
	Repetitions							
Backrest without chair and multibond	Repetitions							
Bouncing strides	Simple Series							
	Hands on head Series							
	Series with charge							
Stretching	Buttock							
	Quadriceps							
	Calves							

Week from..... to.....		Mon	Tues	Wed	Thur	Fri	Sat	Sun
Squat	Mass							
	Series							
	Repetitions							
	Total volume							
Jumping rope	Duration							
Electro Stimulation	Buttock Muscle							
	Quadriceps							
	Calves							
Plank	Repetitions							
	Duration							
8 jumps, sprint 30 m, recover 15″	Repetitions							
10 jumps, maintain 10″	Repetitions							

Week from..... to.....		Mon	Tues	Wed	Thur	Fri	Sat	Sun
Squat hop	*Series*							
Step	*Series*							
	Repetitions							
Thrust up	*Series*							
	Repetitions							
Backrest without chair and multibond	*Repetitions*							
Bouncing strides	*Simple Series*							
	Hands on head Series							
	Series with charge							
Stretching	*Buttock*							
	Quadriceps							
	Calves							

Week from..... to.....		Mon	Tues	Wed	Thur	Fri	Sat	Sun
Squat	Mass							
	Series							
	Repetitions							
	Total volume							
Jumping rope	Duration							
Electro Stimulation	Buttock Muscle							
	Quadriceps							
	Calves							
Plank	Repetitions							
	Duration							
8 jumps, sprint 30 m, recover 15''	Repetitions							
10 jumps, maintain 10''	Repetitions							

Week from..... to.....		Mon	Tues	Wed	Thur	Fri	Sat	Sun
Squat hop	Series							
Step	Series							
	Repetitions							
Thrust up	Series							
	Repetitions							
Backrest without chair and multibond	Repetitions							
Bouncing strides	Simple Series							
	Hands on head Series							
	Series with charge							
Stretching	Buttock							
	Quadriceps							
	Calves							

Week from..... to.....		Mon	Tues	Wed	Thur	Fri	Sat	Sun
Squat	Mass							
	Series							
	Repetitions							
	Total volume							
Jumping rope	Duration							
Electro Stimulation	Buttock Muscle							
	Quadriceps							
	Calves							
Plank	Repetitions							
	Duration							
8 jumps, sprint 30 m, recover 15″	Repetitions							
10 jumps, maintain 10″	Repetitions							

Week from..... to.....		Mon	Tues	Wed	Thur	Fri	Sat	Sun
Squat hop	Series							
Step	Series							
	Repetitions							
Thrust up	Series							
	Repetitions							
Backrest without chair and multibond	Repetitions							
Bouncing strides	Simple Series							
	Hands on head Series							
	Series with charge							
Stretching	Buttock							
	Quadriceps							
	Calves							

Week from..... to.....		Mon	Tues	Wed	Thur	Fri	Sat	Sun
Squat	Mass							
	Series							
	Repetitions							
	Total volume							
Jumping rope	Duration							
Electro Stimulation	Buttock Muscle							
	Quadriceps							
	Calves							
Plank	Repetitions							
	Duration							
8 jumps, sprint 30 m, recover 15"	Repetitions							
10 jumps, maintain 10"	Repetitions							

Week from..... to.....		Mon	Tues	Wed	Thur	Fri	Sat	Sun
Squat hop	*Series*							
Step	*Series*							
	Repetitions							
Thrust up	*Series*							
	Repetitions							
Backrest without chair and multibond	*Repetitions*							
Bouncing strides	*Simple Series*							
	Hands on head Series							
	Series with charge							
Stretching	*Buttock*							
	Quadriceps							
	Calves							

Week from..... to.....		Mon	Tues	Wed	Thur	Fri	Sat	Sun
Squat	Mass							
	Series							
	Repetitions							
	Total volume							
Jumping rope	Duration							
Electro Stimulation	Buttock Muscle							
	Quadriceps							
	Calves							
Plank	Repetitions							
	Duration							
8 jumps, sprint 30 m, recover 15''	Repetitions							
10 jumps, maintain 10''	Repetitions							

Week from..... to.....		Mon	Tues	Wed	Thur	Fri	Sat	Sun
Squat hop	*Series*							
Step	*Series*							
	Repetitions							
Thrust up	*Series*							
	Repetitions							
Backrest without chair and multibond	*Repetitions*							
Bouncing strides	*Simple Series*							
	Hands on head Series							
	Series with charge							
Stretching	*Buttock*							
	Quadriceps							
	Calves							

Week from..... to.....		Mon	Tues	Wed	Thur	Fri	Sat	Sun
Squat	Mass							
	Series							
	Repetitions							
	Total volume							
Jumping rope	Duration							
Electro Stimulation	Buttock Muscle							
	Quadriceps							
	Calves							
Plank	Repetitions							
	Duration							
8 jumps, sprint 30 m, recover 15''	Repetitions							
10 jumps, maintain 10''	Repetitions							

Week from..... to.....		Mon	Tues	Wed	Thur	Fri	Sat	Sun
Squat hop	*Series*							
Step	*Series*							
	Repetitions							
Thrust up	*Series*							
	Repetitions							
Backrest without chair and multibond	*Repetitions*							
Bouncing strides	*Simple Series*							
	Hands on head Series							
	Series with charge							
Stretching	*Buttock*							
	Quadriceps							
	Calves							

Week from..... to.....		Mon	Tues	Wed	Thur	Fri	Sat	Sun
Squat	Mass							
	Series							
	Repetitions							
	Total volume							
Jumping rope	Duration							
Electro Stimulation	Buttock Muscle							
	Quadriceps							
	Calves							
Plank	Repetitions							
	Duration							
8 jumps, sprint 30 m, recover 15"	Repetitions							
10 jumps, maintain 10"	Repetitions							

Week from..... to.....		Mon	Tues	Wed	Thur	Fri	Sat	Sun
Squat hop	Series							
Step	Series							
	Repetitions							
Thrust up	Series							
	Repetitions							
Backrest without chair and multibond	Repetitions							
Bouncing strides	Simple Series							
	Hands on head Series							
	Series with charge							
Stretching	Buttock							
	Quadriceps							
	Calves							

Week from..... to.....		Mon	Tues	Wed	Thur	Fri	Sat	Sun
Squat	Mass							
	Series							
	Repetitions							
	Total volume							
Jumping rope	Duration							
Electro Stimulation	Buttock Muscle							
	Quadriceps							
	Calves							
Plank	Repetitions							
	Duration							
8 jumps, sprint 30 m, recover 15"	Repetitions							
10 jumps, maintain 10"	Repetitions							

Week from..... to.....		Mon	Tues	Wed	Thur	Fri	Sat	Sun
Squat hop	*Series*							
Step	*Series*							
	Repetitions							
Thrust up	*Series*							
	Repetitions							
Backrest without chair and multibond	*Repetitions*							
Bouncing strides	*Simple Series*							
	Hands on head Series							
	Series with charge							
Stretching	*Buttock*							
	Quadriceps							
	Calves							

Week from..... to.....		Mon	Tues	Wed	Thur	Fri	Sat	Sun
Squat	Mass							
	Series							
	Repetitions							
	Total volume							
Jumping rope	Duration							
Electro Stimulation	Buttock Muscle							
	Quadriceps							
	Calves							
Plank	Repetitions							
	Duration							
8 jumps, sprint 30 m, recover 15"	Repetitions							
10 jumps, maintain 10"	Repetitions							

Week from..... to.....		Mon	Tues	Wed	Thur	Fri	Sat	Sun
Squat hop	*Series*							
Step	*Series*							
	Repetitions							
Thrust up	*Series*							
	Repetitions							
Backrest without chair and multibond	*Repetitions*							
Bouncing strides	*Simple Series*							
	Hands on head Series							
	Series with charge							
Stretching	*Buttock*							
	Quadriceps							
	Calves							

Made in the USA
Las Vegas, NV
22 November 2023

81361665R00066